Pride *of* Black British Women

Deborah King

 A **HANSIB** Educational Publication

920.009296

First published in 1995 by Hansib Publishing Limited,
Third Floor, Tower House, 141-149 Fonthill Road London N4 3HF England.

Printed in Malta by Interprint Limited

British Library Cataloguing-In-Publication Data.
A catalogue record for this book is available from the British Library.

ISBN 1-879518-34-9

Acknowledgements

This book is dedicated to my daughter, Mellody Wilson-King. She is my inspiration.

Also, many thanks to Donald Thomas for all his understanding and support.

My thanks and gratitude go to everyone who supported and took part in the work of producing this book.

It is designed to be for all children - who need to know that they are capable of fashioning any career they wish to pursue.

Millions of people have worked hard and endeavoured to make sure that children can have the careers they want.

MAKE SURE YOU HAVE THE CAREER THAT YOU WANT, IT IS YOUR RIGHT.

Deborah King

Contents

Introduction

Role models have always played an essential role in the healthy development of society. They provide positive images for both young people and their peers to aspire to. But traditionally black women have only been portrayed in subordinate roles such as those of maids, kitchen hands or cleaners. During the Second World War, black women were seen as nurses and cooks and, therefore, with the labour migrations from the Caribbean of the 1950s and 60s, black women were indeed assigned jobs as cooks, cleaners, nurses and factory workers.

Black women in the 1980s and 90s have striven to acquire good educations and to progress in their career, but too little of this has been acknowledged.

At present in Britain, young black people look to famous African-Americans, Africans and sometimes Caribbeans for their role models. This is a good start, but young black Britons also need role models who reflect their own specific cross-cultural identity and situation.

Pride of Black British Women has been produced to provide young people, particularly young black people who were born in Britain, with positive images and role models of women who they can relate to, identify with and aspire to emulate.

This book is a collection of profiles, focusing on the educational and career achievements of successful black women in Britain.

Although the women profiled have come from a variety of cultural backgrounds, most were born in Britain, and all identify themselves as "black British women". Their range of careers and educational backgrounds and their words of encouragement, will enable young people to see how others have succeeded, be aware of their own ability to achieve and help them to realise their own career goals.

Foreword

I am delighted that Deborah King has asked me to say a few words about this excellent compilation about the high achieving black women in this country.

I have many invitations to go to schools to speak on speech days and I am very conscious of the gap that exists in the knowledge that children have about what many of us are doing in so many diverse fields. I believe that black women are tremendously dynamic because of the numerous odds they have to face in their struggle to succeed, it is quite remarkable that so many of us do succeed! I hope that Deborah King will realise her ambition to see this book in every school library.

If this book serves to inspire and encourage a few of our young people it will have done a worthwhile service to the black community.

The Rt Hon Baroness Shreela Flather

Diane Abbott, MP

In July 1987 Diane Abbott was elected to the British Parliament at the relatively young age of 33. Serving as the Labour MP for the London constituency of Hackney North and Stoke Newington, she was the first black woman ever elected to the British parliament and one of only forty two women MPs out of a total of six hundred and fifty parliamentarians. Consequently, her election made history and received media attention worldwide.

Ms Abbott's family are originally from the Caribbean island of Jamaica and she maintains strong political links with the country. In 1987 she was awarded the prestigious Ministers Medal of Appreciation for services to the island. She was very involved in relief work for the island in the aftermath of Hurricane Gilbert.

Ms Abbott excelled at school and went on to gain an honours degree in history at Cambridge University.

After graduation she worked for the Home Office as an administrative trainee, becoming the highest ranking black woman employed there at the time.

She went on to work for the long-established National Council for Civil Liberties - now known as Liberty - where she worked as their national race relations officer, playing a leading role in civil rights campaigning.

In 1979 she took up journalism as a career, working in many branches of the media, including public relations, freelance journalism and television.

Her political activity began with many years of work as a grassroots activist in the Labour Party. She also served as a city councillor in Westminster from 1982 to 1986.

In 1987 she received a Hansib Community Award.

Her current political interests are wide and varied. She is particularly concerned about the plight of the poor and minorities. In 1989 she was appointed to the Treasury Select Committee of the House of Commons. This committee has a responsibility to oversee economic affairs. At Labour's 1994

annual conference she was elected to the party's governing National Executive Committee (NEC).

Ms Abbott's constituency has a population of 92,000. It is one of the poorest districts in the whole of Britain, and some 60 per cent of her constituency are black people.

Her ambitions are to continue to serve the people of her constituency and to write a best selling novel.

Dounne Alexander-Moore

Dounne Alexander-Moore was born in the Caribbean nation of Trinidad and Tobago. Her family came to Britain in 1963 and lived in Seven Kings, Essex. She continued her schooling at Canon Palmer school where her favourite subjects were English Literature and the sciences. Her first job was as a laboratory technician, which enabled her to pursue science studies at college. She left after four years to work for a fashion company and after another three years moved on to a housing association. She studied housing management, becoming Britain's first black housing manager.

She married in 1971, had two daughters, and divorced in 1989. She started her food manufacturing business, called Gramma's UK Ltd, in 1987, producing Gramma's Herbal Pepper Sauces. These products are now available in numerous good stores and supermarkets, including Harrods and Selfridges in London.

She has become a very highly-profiled small business-person, having been featured on television more than 40 times, in magazines more than 250 times, as well as in numerous newspapers and books.

Her greatest ambition is to establish a large factory and to see her products in stores worldwide.

At the end of 1993, she received the Jewish Kosher Certificate, which was a first for an African-Caribbean food product.

Valarie Amos

Valarie Amos was born in Guyana, South America, but has lived in Britain most of her life.

Valarie was educated at Warwick , Birmingham and East Anglia Universities.

Currently Chief Executive of the Equal Opportunities Commission, Valarie started her career with the south London Borough of Lambeth in 1981, working as a Race Relations Adviser. She then moved to the north London Borough of Camden where she worked as a Women's Adviser on housing and social services issues.

In 1985 she joined Hackney Council in east London as the borough's head of Training and Development, she then went on to become its Head of Management Services.

The Equal Opportunities Commission is the national sex equality agency. It was established by an act of parliament and is funded by, but independent of, government.

Valarie's other interests include being a director of the Hampstead Theatre, an advisory board member of the BBC, a member of the Kings College Fund Committee, an external examiner for the Universities of Liverpool and Northumbria, an advisory board member of the Centre for Educational Development and Appraisal at the University of Warwick, a Trustee of the Runnymede Trust and the Women's Therapy Centre and an Executive Committee member of the Child Poverty Action Group.

She has written extensively on sex and race discrimination issues and presented numerous papers at national and international conferences.

Jencil Austin

Jencil Austin

Jencil was born in Barbados and came to England when she was seven years old. She attended North Paddington Secondary School where she obtained a number of CSEs.

On leaving school, Jencil went to work as a typist for the National Association of Youth Clubs, where she stayed for around 18 months before being made redundant. She then worked in a variety of places as a 'temp', including a stint at the Department of Employment, before taking up a permanent post as a typist with the Inner London Education Authority (ILEA). She worked in the Educational Welfare Department and found her interest in working with children was getting bigger.

During this period Jencil thought about being a Social Aunt, someone who would befriend young people who lived in childrens' homes. But she did not follow up her interest until many years later.

Jencil took a break from working to give birth to her son. But when she was ready to return to work she found it very difficult to find child care.

She therefore decided to return to study, taking many different courses, including maths, cookery and cake decorating. She also did some bereavement counselling for a period of some two years.

Then Jencil saw an advertisement in the local paper asking for foster carers for children who lived in childrens' homes.

She decided to apply and, after a long assessment process, was approved by Kensington and Chelsea Fostering and Adoption Department as a short-term foster carer.

Jencil has now been fostering for some seven years and in that time she has cared for at least 24 children from many different cultural backgrounds.

Her ambitions are to write her autobiography, have a reunion party for all of the children that she has cared for, become a lay visitor at police stations to ensure that prisoners are being fairly treated and possibly become a magistrate.

Dame Jocelyn Barrow, DBE

Jocelyn Barrow was born in Trinidad and came to England in 1959. She read English at the University of London and holds a postgraduate degree in Education from Furzedown Teachers College. In 1979 she was seconded for three years to the University of London Institute of Education. She was awarded an honorary Doctor of Letters by the University of East London in 1992.

She has served on a great many national and local committees, among them the Taylor Committee on School Governors, as General Secretary (later Vice-Chairwoman) of the Campaign Against Racial Discrimination (1964-69), Vice-Chairwoman of the International Human Rights Year Committee in 1968, Member of the Community Relations Commission (1968-72), Member of the Parole Board (1983-87), National Vice-President of the National Union of Townswomen's Guilds (1978-80, 1987-present). She is a Fellow of the Royal Society of Arts and a Governor of the British Film Institute.

Amongst her current appointments, she is Chairwoman of the Independent Equal Opportunities Inquiry into Ethnicity, Training and Assessment on the Bar Vocational Course, Chairwoman of the Independent Committee of Management of the optical department of the consumer complaints service and a non-executive director of the Whittington Hospital NHS Trust.

Her public work, both of the voluntary and paid kind, has kept her closely in touch with the general public. She was awarded an OBE in 1972 for her contribution to education and community relations, she received a Hansib Community Award in 1988 and was made a Dame of the British Empire (DBE) in 1992.

She is married to barrister Henderson Downer, of Lincoln's Inn and the Jamaican Bar, and lives in central London.

The BiBi Crew

The BiBi Crew was formed in 1991 and consisted of Joanne Campbell, Judith Jacob, Janet Kay (who has since left due to recording commitments), Suzette Llewellyn, Josephine Melville, Beverley Michaels and Suzanne Packer. Each actress has at least 10 years experience in theatre, television, radio and film.

The company is dedicated to producing high quality new writing from an African-Caribbean perspective and to introducing the black British experience to a larger cosmopolitan audience.

Joanne Campbell

Joanne Campbell was born in Northampton. Her mother is Trinidadian and her father is Jamaican.

Joanne attended Northampton High School for Girls. After passing nine 'O' levels, she successfully auditioned and was admitted to the Arts Education College in London. Here she studied dance, drama, singing and 'A' level music and English. In the course of these studies, the opportunity arose for Joanne to join the comedy duo 'Cannon and Ball' on their national tour as lead singer and dancer. Although this meant she would miss her 'A' level examinations she decided to go on the tour, believing that it was too good an opportunity to miss and that she could always sit the exams another time. She is still trying to find that time.

As well as being a founder member of the BiBi Crew, Joanne's other roles include Liz in the comedy series 'Me and My Girl' and Mavis in the childrens' programme 'Bodger & Badger'. She also played Beverly in the first series of Us Girls'.

Her theatre appearances include as Josephine Baker in 'This is my Dream', Amanda Chase in 'Private Lives' and Millie Cubson in 'The Cotton Club'.

Joanne is on the board of directors at the Theatre Royal

Stratford. When she has some spare time, she spends it reading, dancing or weight training, with some aerobics thrown in!

Judith Jacob

Judith's childhood dream was to be an actress. Throughout her primary and secondary school days, she achieved good results academically. She also participated in all the school plays and performed on television.

It was while she was studying for 'A' levels in maths and English that she successfully auditioned for an acting job, which meant having to take the decision to leave school.

Instead of completing her 'A' levels, Judith became the nurse Beverly Slater in the TV series 'Angels'. It was the start of her career as an actress, she later went on to star in 'Eastenders' and 'The Real McKoy'. She decided to take a City and Guilds course in electronics. She received a merit and a distinction in her first year exams, but was not able to continue as she had started working in theatre for the first time which meant that she did not have free evenings. She has, however, fulfiled her childhood dream.

Janet Kay

Janet Kay attended a secondary modern girls school in Kilburn, London. Whilst there she was very involved in music and drama although, at the time, she did not think that she would pursue them as a career.

Rather, upon leaving school Janet took a secretarial course at Watford College, where, following two years' study, she was awarded a diploma with distinction.

In her last term at college, Janet set about looking for a job, which did not prove too difficult as her qualifications for the secretarial post she was looking for were good. She was employed at Roneo Vickers for two years as secretary to the Branch Manager. But it was a fairly small branch and Janet decided to move on. She was then employed by Rank Xerox as a personnel assistant and it was after a year in this job that she became professionally involved in music.

Janet had a few records released that did well in the reggae market, but it was when she recorded and released a track entitled "Silly Games" in 1980 that things really changed. The record became a National Chart No.1 hit and it was at this point that Janet gave up her routine job, although she continued to do some temporary work from time to time.

It was also around this time that Janet became involved in drama, being given a part in one of the Black Theatre Co-operative's first plays, the musical 'Mama Dragon'.

With very hard work, Janet has gone from strength to strength in both music and drama. She has released an album entitled "Love You Always" in Japan and her success in the record industry has meant she has had to leave the BiBi Crew.

Janet is very interested in the knitwear industry and recently completed her two-year City and Guilds in Machine Knitting Design. When time permits, she sells her one-off designs.

Suzette Llewellyn

Becoming an actress was not something that Suzette Llewellyn had really planned. Although she had been a member of the Cockpit and National Youth Theatres, when it came to discussing careers, she was not sure how she saw her future. Her favourite subjects at school were history, English and art and, encouraged by her English teacher, she successfully applied for drama school. After completing three years at drama school she was able to expand her knowledge of her favourite subjects, but from the perspective of a black woman.

She was fortunate in that before leaving drama school she was offered both a job, as Viola in 'Twelfth Night', and an agent.

Although she found her first year in the profession wonderful, the second was spent doing a variety of jobs that had nothing whatsoever to do with acting. That was her worst year, but it did teach her that waiting for the telephone to ring with a job offer was not the best way to spend your life.

In trying to create work for herself, she joined writing groups, performed her own poetry and led drama classes, before finally becoming a co-founder of the BiBi Crew.

Suzette says: "My parents always said you should have something to fall back on. They're right. Your fate is in your hands."

Josephine Melville

Josephine was born and brought up in London, with both her parents coming from Jamaica.

She went to Stratford Comprehensive School in east London, where she gained five CSEs as well as an 'O' level in English.

Having studied dance at an early age, Josephine was in no doubt that she wanted to enter the entertainment business. However, her parents were adamant that she should have a back-up career and advised her to go to college. She went to East London College of Technology and took a shorthand and secretarial course. However, she was already hooked on the stage and her hobby became her profession.

Having performed in theatres all over England as well as abroad, Josephine has found that being in the entertainment business has enabled her to travel to countries that previously she only ever saw in books, and when she is not working as an actress, her secretarial abilities enable her to do temporary work. She also finds that her secretarial qualifications are useful for all the administration duties that are needed within the BiBi Crew. Being both an actress and a company director, Josephine feels that her dream has become a reality.

The conclusion she draws from this is: "Never lose sight of your dreams. But make sure you are equipped to carry them through."

Beverley Michaels

While still at school, Beverley became restless with 'playing out' and was keen to get involved with other things. A friend of hers attended drama class after school and suggested that she came along. Although she was not sure what to expect, she felt sure that it would be more interesting than how she was spending her time at the moment.

She attended Anna Scher (a school for performing arts and drama) after school twice a week and got increasingly involved in acting. This led to offers of appearing on television and getting time off school to film, although she still had to do school work during quiet moments on set. Always intending to continue her education, Beverley decided to stay on to the sixth form and do 'A' levels. But while she was still at school the opportunity arose to appear in a film, which she accepted. She left the sixth form knowing that at some stage in her life she would return to study. It took her seven years to return, however, she has obtained a BEd (Hons) in Speech and Drama, enabling her to teach drama and English at secondary level. Beverley says that: "Studying has allowed me to be more disciplined in getting closer to my aspirations in life. It has also helped me to develop and enhance skills I already had, but didn't quite know how to utilise. It is my own personal achievement in life that no-one can ever take away from me because I have earned and worked hard for it.

The BiBi Crew allows her to be flexible, working either as an actress or a school teacher. "My parents and teachers encouraged me to have another career I could 'fall back on', because acting can be very precarious, although at the time, being young and inexperienced, it seemed that I wouldn't have the time to do both, but I eventually found the time and still I smile about it now, when I think of the freedom education has given me."

Suzanne Packer

As a child, Suzanne had aspirations to be a journalist as she loved reading and the sound and 'feel' of words - as indeed she still does. In school her natural leaning was towards the arts. She passed nine 'O' levels at age 16, including maths, German, biology and music. She went on to pass three 'A' levels - in English, history and French. Even though she played a lot of sports, including netball and athletics, in which she represented the school, school plays and musicals became a greater love.

She became a member of the National Youth Theatre of Wales and sang with the South Glamorgan County Choir. She also played second violin with the South Glamorgan Youth Orchestra.

After her 'A' levels, Suzanne went on to Warwick University, where she obtained a BA in Theatre Studies and Dramatic Art. Then, after just two terms at the Webber Douglas Academy of Dramatic Art, studying for a diploma in acting, Suzanne got her first job, with a much-prized Equity union card, in a production called 'Tithe' at the Unicorn Theatre for children.

Since then, she has widened her experience in the theatre greatly by working in musicals, opera, radio, theatre, comedy and television.

ROW (l-r): Beverley Michaels, Suzette Llewellyn, Joanne Campbell. FRONT ROW (l-r): Josephine Melville, Suzanne Packer, Judith Jacob

Cheryl Burden

Cheryl Burden

Cheryl Burden was in what she describes as a 'township of Manchester called Chorlton-cum-Hardy'.

From the age of 11 she attended Loreto College in Manchester, leaving school at the age of 18 having obtained nine 'O' levels and three 'A' levels. Whilst at school she represented Greater Manchester in athletics and was also a member of the Manchester Youth Orchestra.

She won a place at Aston University in Birmingham, where, in 1984, she graduated with an honours degree in chemistry. Whilst at university she applied for, and was accepted by, the Metropolitan Police Service.

After initial training at Hendon Police College which lasted 20 weeks she was posted to Harrow Road Police station in West London.

She spent five years at this station, the majority of this time as a relief officer. In 1990 she sat the Sergeant's Promotion examination and passed on the first attempt. Later that year she was posted to Romford Police station and is currently serving at a satellite station, Harold Hill, where she is in charge of a small team of six police officers.

Cheryl has been married for six years to a research chemist and they have one son who was born in November 1992.

She returned to work after a short period of maternity leave and shortly afterwards passed both parts of the Inspector's examination.

"I am proud to be a police officer and can see this being my career for life. I hope to achieve the highest rank possible during my time in the service,". said Cheryl. "I strongly believe that more minority officers are required in the service to make it truly representative of the community that we serve in the metropolis".

Maxine Chandler

Maxine was born in London. She went to St Marks school in south London where she obtained five GCSEs.

Deciding that she wanted to go into carpentry, she went to college with a view to taking a two year City and Guilds course in carpentry and joinery. After attending the course for some time, Maxine decided to leave to get some work experience, which she did for some six months. After this, a job opportunity came up as a furniture stripper in Bradford. Maxine did this job for about nine months and during this period she was also given the opportunity to train as a furniture restorer. After this, Maxine returned to London to complete her City and Guilds course.

While at college Maxine did quite a lot of voluntary work at youth clubs. She enjoyed the work so much that at one stage she thought that she might work with people as a career by becoming a social worker. However, in the end Maxine decided that she preferred to be a carpenter.

On finishing college, Maxine decided to start her own business, for which she received funding from the Prince's Youth Business Trust and the Economic Development Unit of the London Borough of Hammersmith and Fulham.

This funding enabled her to get her own tools, equipment and van.

Maxine is enjoying running her own business and watching her ambitions grow. In five years time, she aims to have her own firm of women carpenters, electricians and so on.

She is also interested in writing a book and in computer programming and travelling.

However, Maxine's greatest ambition is to open her own furniture restoration shop in Europe.

Maxine suffers from dyslexia, but she believes that if you are positive and confident about yourself, nothing can stop you from achieving what you want in life.

Photo courtesy: Richard Reyes

Winsome-Grace Cornish

Winsome Cornish joined the *Voice* newspaper as a freelance publicist in 1983, initially to launch a provincial publicity campaign aimed at increasing awareness of the newspaper outside the capital.

Her work at The Voice Communications Group has seen her handle a wide variety of projects within the group prior to her appointment as editor in 1990.

She was editor of the monthly women's interest magazine, Chic, and subsequently edited the *Voice* colour supplement - *VS Magazine*.

She co-managed songstress Mica Paris, helping to launch the soulster's successful music career, and was a researcher for the popular LWT programme 'Club Mix'.

Winsome's background prior to joining the *Voice* was mainly in public relations. She started as a press officer for United Artist Records, where she organised publicity for a wide range of artists covering pop, punk, reggae and rock.

Winsome is a self-taught journalist and firmly believes that with sufficient interest and endeavour 'the world is every woman's oyster'.

Marie Cunningham

Marie Cunningham was born in Britain but completed her education in Jamaica where she obtained a BA degree in communications and social sciences from the University of the West Indies.

She also has a Technical Teachers Certificate from Wimbledon Technical College and has received awards from music and drama colleges.

Marie is a senior partner at CPW Associates, which is a firm of training consultants providing training in communication and business skills and community relations, as well as consultancy services in business development, export marketing, and equal opportunities and recruitment.

She has worked extensively in the media, having been both a freelance journalist and a TV presenter. Marie has also been a managing director for The Voice Communications Group. This involved having responsibility for general administration, 60 members of staff, public affairs and marketing strategy. Whilst in this position she initiated middle management training and the circulation of the newspaper increased by 30 per cent in her first two years, with the upward trend continuing.

Marie is also involved in many community organisations. She is a committee member of the South Thames Training and Enterprise Council and is on the steering group for the Brixton City Challenge.

Brenda Emmanus

Brenda was born in South London to parents who arrived in Britain from St. Lucia in the 1960s. She has a younger sister and two brothers. She went to a Roman Catholic secondary school successfully completing 'O' and 'A' levels, before applying to what was then the Polytechnic of Central London (now Westminster University).

She studied for a BA in Media Studies, but while doing that she also freelanced as a journalist for various publications, mainly the *Voice* newspaper. She also compered various community and charity shows, and got involved in dance groups and other black community organisations.

Immediately on completing her degree, she joined the *Voice* as a news reporter, expanding her duties to include arts and entertainment reporting. She also worked as a music journalist for 'Black Beat International' music magazine, which was part of The Voice Communications Group.

A couple of years later the same company started *Chic* Magazine, which was designed to be a woman's magazine. Brenda became the features editor and also had responsibility for their arts and entertainment pages. She continued to freelance during this time. This included work for the BBC on the black magazine programme 'Ebony', where Brenda was a freelance researcher and reporter.

When the BBC started the current affairs debate show 'Kilroy', Brenda applied and was accepted as a researcher. Since then her television career has included; Breakfast Time, BBC Youth Programmes, Travelogue for Channel 4 and the Clothes Show, which she is currently presenting, while continuing to freelance. Her work includes compering shows, presenting awards, recording radio adverts, freelance writing for a variety of publications and developing programme ideas for future production.

Baroness Shreela Flather

Lady Flather came to this country as a student from India in 1952. She received her training in law from University College London and the Inner Temple, but rather than pursuing a career in law, she became a teacher in London. She moved to Maidenhead in 1957 and secured a job as a teacher of English as a Second Language for Asian boys at a secondary modern school.

The turning point in her life came in an interview with the headmaster, who told her that he had two problems with her: one that she was a women and secondly, as he put it, "you are not one of us." She encountered blatant racism within the school and was shocked by the treatment received by the Asian children. She was then instrumental in setting up a mother and toddler group for Asian women, followed shortly by a club for Asian boys and a summer school project for Asian children. Through this voluntary work, she became involved in the local community and became a magistrate in 1971.

In 1976 she became the first ethnic minority woman councillor in Britain and in 1986 she became Britain's first Asian woman mayor - for the Royal Borough of Windsor and Maidenhead. The same year she received a Hansib Community Award. She has been active in the Conservative Party throughout this period and has served on numerous public bodies, including the Committee of the Race Relations Board and subsequently on the Commission for Racial Equality. She is also a governor of the Commonwealth Institute.

She has campaigned tirelessly to improve race relations and was herself the victim of a horrific racial attack in 1971 when a very heavy iron bar was thrown into her house, narrowly missing her son, and racist graffiti was daubed all over her walls.

Since entering the House of Lords she has been able to strengthen Clause 95 of the Criminal Justice Act 1991 by making it a duty for everyone involved in the criminal justice system to avoid discriminating on racial grounds. This measure was supported by peers from all sides of the House.

Pride of Black British Women

Jacqui Harper

Jacqui was born in Ilkley, Yorkshire, spending her early childhood in Bradford, before moving to east London at the age of seven.

She passed her 'O' and 'A' levels at school and went on to study at Sussex University, where she was awarded a BA degree in English and American Literature. She successfully obtained her master's degree in mass communications from the University of Westminster.

She has worked extensively in the media and has been a journalist, reporter and presenter, including both BBC TV and ITV. She was the presenter of 'Advice Shop' and was the talk show host of 'Hearsay', a half-hour topical show with guests and a studio audience.

Jacqui has worked as a TV presenter for GMTV and now she is a presenter for Network Southeast for the BBC, which provides national and international news updates as well as live interviews. As a travel correspondent, she has covered destinations worldwide for GMTV's series, 'Holiday Snaps' and she presents 'Timeshift' - a weekly review of top stories.

Outside work, Jacqui takes an active part in educational projects aimed at encouraging young people to fulfil their dreams. She has previously acted as a mentor to students at North London College (now the University of North London) and lectured at various schools and colleges in the capital.

Her great ambitions include wanting to meet Nelson Mandela and to write a novel.

Marian Harrison

Marian was born in London. Her mother is English and her father is from West Africa.

She went to school in Willesden and from there went on to the London School of Fashion, where she was awarded a City and Guilds in dressmaking, pattern cutting and design.

Her first job was as a design room assistant, but she did not stay there long as she wanted to gain greater and wider experience with different companies. A number of the earlier companies she worked for supplied high street stores. However, Marian's ambition was to work on exclusive clothing and she eventually managed to get a job in a fashion house, where she learned how to sew high class garments.

After many years of training and full-time work, she decided to start her own business. In 1990 she approached the North West London Business Support Initiative and took a short course. Marian was then able to start her own business in 1991 with the help of the enterprise allowance scheme. She now runs a small dressmaking company, which offers personal service and has a good turnover. She is, of course, hoping to expand and remarks:

"I enjoy the freedom and self-satisfaction that comes from being your own boss."

Delia Jarrette-Macauley

Delia was born in Hertfordshire, England and went to school in Yorkshire. She attended York College for Girls and Harrogate Grammar School where she obtained her 'O' levels and 'A' levels. She then went to London University where she obtained her first degree in management and later was awarded a PhD in English.

After leaving university, Delia worked in the arts for various organisations, including the Minority Arts Advisory Service, Greater London Arts and the Black Dance Development Trust.

Delia has also done a lot of management training and consultancy work.

In 1989, she began to teach Womens' Studies at Kent University at MA level. Delia has also written and edited several books. They include:

The Biography of Una Marson, 1905-1965.

A Collection of Una Marson's Writings.

An Anthology of Writings by Women about Black Women in Britain.

Her latest book, called *Reconstructing Womenhood, Reconstructing Feminism*, is being published by Routledge.

Delia's lifetime ambitions are varied: She would like to develop good quality relationships with people; learn to understand herself and the world better; and would also like to continue writing.

Joan Yvette Moore

Joan's parents emigrated to this country from Barbados in the early 60's and she was born in Hammersmith, west London. The family lived in Cricklewood until Joan was seven, when they moved to Harrow where she has lived ever since.

Having obtained her 'O' and 'A' levels, Joan went to Trent Polytechnic, Nottingham, where in 1985, she graduated with a law degree. She took the Bar finals the following year and has now been a practising barrister for more than seven years.

Joan advises and represents clients at court in all aspects of family law, including children, divorce and domestic violence.

She is currently on the Executive Committee of the Harrow Council for Racial Equality and is a member of the Society of Black Lawyers and the Harrow African-Caribbean Association.

In the past she has assisted in the running of supplementary classes for children and young adults at a local community centre, giving legal advice at the local law centre, and, as a student was the President of the African-Caribbean Society and Vice-President of Lincoln's Inn Students Union.

If she remains at the Bar, her ambition would be to obtain a judicial appointment. Otherwise, she would like to reach a position where she could be influential in the decision-making process affecting the community. On a personal level, she would like to be able to perform a cartwheel!

Usha Kumari Prashar

Usha was born in Kenya. Committed to developing good race relations, she has a BA degree in political science from the University of Leeds, as well as a Diploma in social administration from the University of Glasgow.

Between 1977-1984, she was the director of the Runnymede Trust, which is concerned with the development of policy and practice in the field of race and immigration. In this position, she was responsible for managing and directing the work of the trust, raising funds, commissioning and undertaking research, as well as communicating and liaising with a wide range of organisations and individuals.

Between 1986-1991, she was the Director of the National Council for Voluntary Organisations (NCVO), in which post she raised funds, managed 150 members of staff and had responsibility for a budget of approximately £3 million. Developing a clearer focus and direction for the NCVO's work, she built effective links with member organisations, government and other sections of society. Her work earned her a Hansib Community Award in 1988.

She is currently involved in a variety of activities, including being a member of the Royal Commission on Criminal Justice, a member of the Lord Chancellor's Advisory Committee on Legal Education and Conduct, and a non-executive director of Channel 4 Television.

Usha has written several books, including *Need for Reform; Sickle Cell Anaemia, Who Cares?* and *Legal Services for Asylum-Seekers*. She has also prepared numerous submissions to Parliamentary Select Committees, written articles for journals and presented papers at international conferences in Europe, the United States and Canada.

Her interests are current affairs, music, visual arts, country walks and squash. More recently she has taken up golf.

Photo courtesy: Joanne O'Brien

Photo courtesy: Sharron Wallace

Beverley Randall

Beverley was born in London. She was educated at St Judes Primary and Dick Shepherd Secondary School in Brixton and on leaving school with modest qualifications went to work for the bankers Coutt's & Co., where she stayed for six years.

She started out as a typist, but by the time she left she was secretary and personal assistant to the sub-manager.

The six years at the bank gave Beverley the time to think about what she really wanted to do. She left Coutt's in 1983 and went to work for the Black Theatre Co-operative. She started as a trainee administrative assistant but rose to be the general manager.

Beverley then went to work at Riverside Studios as a programme co-ordinator. She gained a great deal of experience before leaving to work for Monkey Game's Productions - which is now called APC Productions - as their director. The company produced programmes such as the '291 Club', the 'Chef' and 'In Dream'.

At present Beverley is producing a Series for the 'POSSE' to be shown on Channel 4.

Her lifetime ambitions are to get better at all the things she does and to work with her sister Paulette Randell on a big project, such as a film. Until now they have never worked together.

Beverley believes that everyone should take the time to think about what they really want to do; because, as she puts it, it is not where you start that matters but where you end up that counts.

Paulette Randall

Paulette was born in London, at Kings College Hospital. She attended St Judes Primary and Dick Shepherd Secondary School in Brixton. Having obtained her 'O' levels she started studying for her 'A' levels but did not complete the course, deciding instead to enrol at the Rose Bruford School of Speech and Drama in Kent. Paulette trained to be an actress for three years and during this period she became one of the four founders of the Theatre of Black Women, who wrote and performed their own work. She also won the 'Young Writers Festival Award' from the Royal Court Theatre for her play 'Fishing'.

Paulette became very interested in directing productions, so she decided to apply for a bursary to study this aspect of dramatic arts. The bursary she was awarded enabled her to study Directing at the Royal Court, where she acted as an Assistant Director to Max Stafford-Clark for a little over a year.

Paulette then went to the Octagon Theatre in Lancashire for a further year, to work as a Director in a Repertory Theatre where she gained a lot of experience.

She then returned to London where she became a Freelance Director. These are some of the plays that she has directed:

'24 Per Cent' (About the percentage of black women in British prisons)

'Piano Lesson' - Written by August Wilson

'Pincy and Kobi' - Written by the Posse

'Pe Cong' - Written by Steve Carter

'Headrock' (This play is about the treatment of women in special hospitals and is written by Sarah Daniels)

Paulette has also been a Consultant Director on a Lenny Henry tour, and was at one time the sole producer of the popular TV series, 'Desmonds'.

Her lifetime ambitions are to improve her scriptwriting, directing and producing and she would also like to write and direct her own film.

Beverley Marie Richards

Beverley was born in England. She went to Willesden High School, London, and after obtaining a number of CSE's went to Paddington College, where she did an RSA secretarial course as well as an English language 'O' level.

After leaving college, Beverley went to work at Marks & Spencers. She started in the secretarial pool, where she learnt their secretarial systems. When Beverley had gained this experience she went to work for the managers of various departments. This included six years working in Marks & Spencers' legal department solely for one solicitor, as well as a stint as an executive secretary in the technical department.

After the birth of her daughter, Beverley returned to work as a department manager's secretary. She is very happy in this position as it gives her the time she needs for her family commitments.

Beverley's lifetime ambitions are to have a nice comfortable home for her family and to go on lots of holidays.

Sade

Sade Adv was born in Ibadan, Nigeria. She left Nigeria with her mother and brother when she was four and came to live in Essex, England where she grew up and went to school.

After leaving school at 15, Sade attended an art school in Colchester where she took a two year sampler course. After choosing to specialise in fashion, she was accepted to study at St Martin's School of Art in London. She graduated three years later with a BA and teamed up with another ex-St Martin's student, to produce clothes that they sold to small shops in London.

Around this time, Sade, as a favour, started singing with some friends who had a band. Although she did not officially classify herself as a singer, it became known in her circle that she was, and Sade was approached by a band, who made the kind of music that she liked, to sing backing vocals.

After two years trying unsuccessfully to secure a record deal, the group split up. Some of the remaining members stayed together and, with Sade as the lead singer, they where signed to Epic Records in 1984. Sade then had two hit records which became chart toppers; 'Smooth Operator' and 'Your love is King'.

Sade still performs with the same musicians now as she did then.

Her intention is to continue making music - she feels it is a craft in which you never stop learning and never stop enjoying, in the hope also that you bring some joy to others. Sade is in the process of bringing out an album of her greatest hits.

Tessa Sanderson, MBE

Tessa Sanderson was awarded the MBE by the Queen in 1985 in recognition of her services to sport. The same year she was given a Hansib Community Award. She also holds an Honorary Fellowship from the Polytechnic of Wolverhampton (now the University of Wolverhampton) and an Honorary Masters Degree from Birmingham University.

Her promotional activities include presenting and appearing on network television and radio. In 1988 Tessa worked for two and a half years as a sports presenter for Sky News.

In 1992 she was honoured by the Variety Club with an award for services to sport and for her work with various charities. In particular, Tessa has become increasingly involved with charitable work for the Variety Club, Great Ormond Street Hospital, and the Paul Orgorman Leukaemia Fund.

In 1993 she launched her own designer leisure wear and exercise video under the title "Body Blitz".

Tessa was voted "Athlete of the Year" for three years by the Sports Writers' Association and "Sports Personality of the Year" by the Athletics Writers' Association.

Her athletics career can be summarised as follows;

1973	1st representative competition for Great Britain.
1976	UK Record - Javelin
1976	Olympics, Montreal - Javelin
1978	Commonwealth Games Gold Medallist - Javelin
1978	European Silver Medallist - Javelin
1980	Olympics, Moscow - Javelin
1981	British & Commonwealth Record - Heptathlon
1983	British & Commonwealth Record - Javelin
1984	Olympic Gold Medallist, Los Angeles - Javelin
1986	Commonwealth Gold Medallist & Record - Javelin
1987	World Championships, Rome - Javelin
1988	Olympics, Seoul - Javelin
1990	Commonwealth Gold Medallist - Javelin
1991	Europa Gold Medallist - Javelin
1992	Olympics, Barcelona - Javelin (4th place)
1992	World Cup, Cuba - Javelin (represented Europe - 1st place)

Rianna Scipio

Rianna's parents migrated from Guyana to Britain in the late 1950s and she was born in London. Her secondary education was not 'conventional' in that her early energy was expended in a life which would take most people up to the age of 30 instead of 16. By 1985, she was a fashion model and she also did freelance make-up on fashion shoots. However, at the age of 20, she decided to go back to college, where she studied for 'A' levels in communications and dance. In her spare time she was lead singer for a group which played at the Albany Empire and the Bass Clef.

Following her 'A' level studies, Rianna did some research work on a local community video about pirate radio and, following this, she managed to get a regular DJ spot on a pirate radio station. She says she enjoyed doing the 'Drive Time' show on Fresh FM, and she started to extend the show by including interviews as a regular feature. Amongst the artists she interviewed were Grover Washington Jnr, Freddie McGregor, Maxi Priest, and the Temptations. She then converted her radio interviews into print articles which were published in journals such as Style and Root.

Encouragement from family and friends led her to think about presenting for television and she applied to the BBC's African Caribbean Programmes Unit for the post of programmes researcher. She was not successful at first, but kept up contact and after a year long wait was eventually accepted on a six month contract. Once this hurdle was crossed, she swiftly progressed from being a television researcher to presenter. Rianna now presents the weather on LWT.

Her ambitions include becoming a novelist and obtaining a university degree. She juggles her time between work, full-time study and being a mother to her daughter, believing that the two main keys to success lie in the things we do in our spare time and in the choices we make along the way. She also believes that with confidence and hard work anything and everything is possible - and she intends to prove it.

Patricia Scotland, QC

Patricia was born in Dominica. At an early age she came to England, where she was educated. She obtained a law degree from London and was called to the Bar in 1977, at Middle Temple, where she was awarded a scholarship. Patricia was also a founder member of 1 Gray's Inn Square Chambers.

She has gained extensive experience in general common law practice, including specialising in family law, especially that with an international aspect; as well as local government and planning, judicial reviews, professional negligence and misconduct, employment, mental health and personal injury.

Patricia also has experience of conducting public and private inquiries, including those regarding professional conduct and disciplinary matters.

Her legal work has often centred around cases involving children and has included international child abduction and child abuse cases. She has represented parties in the Jasmine Beckford, Tyra Henry and Kimberley Carlile child abuse inquiries.

Patricia is currently leading an inquiry, under Section 28 of the Housing Act 1985, into the affairs of an housing association.

She is a regular speaker and participant at conferences, both in Britain and abroad, on international affairs, family law and mental health.

Patricia has also been a presenter and participant on various television and radio programmes dealing with environmental, legal and religious issues.

She is married to a fellow member of the Bar and is the mother of a young son.

Patricia's interests are her family, music and literature, the church, sports, world travel and charity work.

Irene Shelley

Irene was born in Lagos, Nigeria. Her parents emigrated to Britain in 1963 and she has been here ever since.

She grew up in Basingstoke, Hampshire, where she attended the Vyne Comprehensive School, gaining six 'O' levels, including French, English and art. Irene then transferred to Queen Mary's Sixth Form College, where she passed 'A' levels in English and art.

In 1979 she attended Winchester School of Art, where she completed a foundation course. From 1980 to 1983, she attended Ravensbourne College of Art and Design, from where she obtained a BA in fashion design. Having enjoyed the course tremendously, she applied to do an MA in fashion at St Martin's School of Art (now Central St Martin's) in central London. She left college finally in 1985, armed with an MA in fashion design and business studies.

After a period as a freelance designer, she applied for a job as fashion editor at *Root* Magazine. She found this work very different from fashion design and she suddenly had to learn about such things as dealing with photographers, models and fashion press offices. Also, she learnt the importance of getting copy in on time and she particularly enjoyed writing articles. Irene stayed at *Root* Magazine for over three years. In 1987, she applied for the job as editor of *Black Beauty & Hair* magazine, and despite her comparative lack of journalistic experience, she was successful.

She has learnt most of her journalistic skills 'on the job', where she is responsible for putting the magazine together. Irene finds her job "fun and very enjoyable", adding that she has had to become more organised and has had to acquire managerial skills.

Eventually she would love to be able to write novels. Indeed, she has already completed one, but it is yet to be published.

Linda Thomlinson

Linda was born in Trinidad and came to England when she was six years old.

After leaving school, Linda went to Paddington College, where she obtained her 'O' levels, and then studied for her 'A' levels by means of a correspondence course.

Linda then worked at a number of jobs, including for NatWest Bank and the housing department of Camden Council.

She returned to education in 1973, taking a three year course at a teacher training college.

In 1977 Linda began her career as a teacher. She worked in a variety of different schools, including St Augustine's Secondary School.

In 1986 Linda was appointed as the deputy head teacher in a London Borough of Brent school, and then, in 1988, she became the head teacher of Wembley Manor Junior School.

However, in 1990 Linda started her own school, which was based in her home. In 1992, she moved the school to a building called Scotts House in Harlesden, north-west London. Her school provides an education for children between the ages of 3-12, specialising in languages.

Linda opened the school to teach "our children in our own way" so they can reach their own aims and goals. She feels that this can only be achieved through our own educational system.

Her ambitions are to make sure that the school is a success and that it outlives her. She would also like to travel round the whole of Africa and retire somewhere warm.

Sharron Wallace

Sharron discovered photography for the first time as a teenager on a holiday playscheme. She was excited and fascinated with the idea of developing black and white prints. She would watch intrigued as the images developed into a photograph and it was then that she decided that she wanted to become a photographer. If nothing else, it seemed a better career option than typing!

At her school there were no lessons in photography, but she was so keen that she photographed the other students. She asked her science teachers to help with the developing and printing.

On leaving school she completed a one year City and Guilds in photography. From there she progressed and worked as a colour printer for four years. She started taking photographs again during this period and contacted various newspapers, particularly black newspapers that she saw her mum reading. She introduced herself and soon found that she was busy, being assigned to take photographs at various functions.

Six months later she was offered a job on the *Voice* newspaper as a picture editor/photographer and is still working there now.

Her work involves taking photographs of people in all walks of life. It might be a photograph of a local man badly beaten by police, a photograph of the prime minister of Jamaica, or a photograph of Whitney Houston.

It's all in a day's work. Forty minutes after one such assignment, she could be photographing marchers on a demonstration protesting the death of Rolan Adams, or a local black family who have just lost their home in a fire.

Being a news photographer requires a great deal of energy for the long hours worked, good communication skills as you're always meeting or photographing people in a variety of situations, a creative approach to work and a ability to work under pressure and to tight deadlines.

The rewards are many, such as the versatility of the work, the opportunities to meet new people and, of course, the chance to take really good photographs.

Any young person wishing to get into photography should aim to get as much experience as possible. Many companies welcome young people on work experience, which not only helps to develop skills, but can also open many doors. Perseverance is the key.

Sharron's advice is to: "believe in yourself, get lots of experience, be confident about putting yourself forward and look for ways of creating opportunities for yourself."

Yvonne Williams

Yvonne was born in Jamaica. She emigrated to Birmingham, England, in June 1968 where she joined her parents. She has a diploma in youth and community work, a certified qualification in social work (CQSW) and a BA degree.

When Yvonne had just finished her course in youth and community work she was interested in a possible career in the probation service. However, she became so tired of trying to find a good hairdressers that she decided to open her own salon. Indeed, she has opened salons both in Birmingham, in April 1984, and in the prestigious Mayfair in central London, in February 1980.

Yvonne learnt everything she knows about hairdressing from 'on the job' experience and from reading books on owning and running your own business.

Her ambition is to see her business expand throughout Europe.

Pride of Black British Women

Quiz

The quiz is designed to get everyone thinking about the professional achievements of black women in Britain.

Guidelines:

- The quiz is more fun if it is played in a group or with more than one person.
- Take it in turns to guess the answer to each question.
- Answer by choosing either a, b or c.
- Write down your answers on a piece of paper.
- Answer all of the questions before checking your answers.
- Then find out the answers from the quiz answers list. Add up each score and see who has won.

1. How many African-Caribbean women do you think are nurses?
   a. 18,000
   b. 20,924
   c. 21,200

2. There are 2,204 African-Caribbean teachers. How many Asian teachers do you think there are in Britain?
   a. 3,000
   b. 1,500
   c. 2,198

3. The total amount of Asian and African-Caribbean secretaries in Britain is 15,310. How many African-Caribbean women do you think are secretaries?
   a. 7,966
   b. 7,344
   c. 7,000

4. How many Asian women solicitors, barristers and judges do you think there are in total?
   a. 2,000
   b. 100
   c. 1,122

5. How many African-Caribbean and Asian woman doctors do you think there are working in Britain?
   a. 1,500
   b. 2,154
   c. 2,863

6. In total there are 17,005 Asian and African Caribbean sewers and embroiderers in Britain. How many Asian women do you think there are?
   a. 2,988
   b. 14,017
   c. 10,000

7. How many African Caribbean women do you think are school helpers?
   a. 1,000
   b. 3,500
   c. 5,599

8. How many Asian women do you think are shop owners/managers?
   a. 15,500
   b. 13,351
   c. 6,450

9. In total there are 1,662 African-Caribbean and Asian restaurant owners. How many African-Caribbean women restaurant owners do you think there are?
   a. 5,000
   b. 1,083
   c. 894

10. How many Asian and African-Caribbean women do you think are electrical/electronic assemblers in total?
    a. 1,202
    b. 2,884
    c. 4,086

11. Do you think you can have any career you want?
    a. YES
    b. YES
    c. YES

ANSWERS TO QUIZ

1. *c*
2. *c*
3. *a*
4. *c*
5. *c*
6. *a*
7. *c*
8. *b*
9. *b*
10. *c*
11. *a, b and c*

Other titles by Hansib

Forthcoming

HIDDEN HEROES - The colonial contribution to the victory over fascism. By John Oakes. Highlighting the contribution of soldiers from African, Asian and Caribbean nations to World War II whose sacrifices; despite Winston Churchill describing their efforts as "crucial to victory"; are largely unsung. Aimed at the general reader, Hidden Heroes will also be of great interest to the military or social historian and can also be used by students as a guide to project sources.
ISBN 1-870519-43-8 Paperback £14.95
(Publication date May 1995)

FROM COLONY TO NATION: THE RISE OF WESTINDIAN CRICKET. By Frank Birbalsingh. Mixing historical reflection with cricket reminiscence to conjure up the magical evocation of the events, issues, attitudes and personalities central to the evolution of Westindian cricket in its most critical years, from the 1920s to the 1960s.
ISBN 1-870518-47-0 Paperback £12.95
(Publication date May 1995)

THE IDEOLOGY OF RACISM. By Samuel Kennedy Yeboah. Reprinted due to popular demand, this comprehensive and well-researched study of the history of peoples from the African diaspora, lists the outstanding achievements in the fields of arts, science and technology as well as trying to tackle the nature of racism
ISBN 1-870518-07-1 Paperback £11.95
(Publication date May 1995)

THE CARIBBEAN - Jamaica, Trinidad and Tobago, Guyana, Barbados. By Steve Garner. A popular and accessible reference work for secondary school students, undergraduates, teachers and the general reader aimed at introducing the major English-speaking countries of the Caribbean to a British audience. Information on history, culture, politics, economics and prominent citizens is given.
ISBN 1-870518-55-1 Paperback, £TBA
(Publication date TBA)

PIONEERS OF PROGRESS - Legendary figures from Africa, Asia and the Americas who changed the course of Social and Political History. By Chris Johnson. A wide ranging collection of essays introducing the contributions of 38 prominent political thinkers and cultural pioneers from the world's non-European majority. Profiles, spanning 250 years, include Toussaint l'Ouverture, Mary Seacole, Mahatma Gandhi, Martin Luther King, Paul Robeson and Bob Marley.
ISBN 1-870518-32-2 Paperback £7.95
(Publication date TBA)

ARISING FROM BONDAGE: A History of East Indians in the Caribbean 1838-1993. By Ron Ramdin. A work of historical research that puts into context the epic story of East Indians in the Caribbean. The book introduces many aspects, both historical and contemporary, of Indian Caribbean history and culture, filling a log-standing gap in Caribbean historiography.
ISBN 1-870518-36-5 Paperback £12.95
(Publication date TBA)

Backlist titles

THE OTHER MIDDLE PASSAGE: Journal of a Voyage from Calcutta to Trinidad, 1858. Introduced by Ron Ramdin. This book reproduces in facsimile the Journal of the captain of a ship carrying indentured labour to the Westindies. The document is put into context by a brief but detailed introductory analysis, highlighting the suffering of this little known mass migration.
ISBN 1-870518-28-4 Paperback £3.95

A NEW SYSTEM OF SLAVERY - The Export of Indian Labour Overseas 1830-1920. By Hugh Tinker. The first comprehensive historical survey of a hitherto neglected and only partially known migration- the export of Indians to supply the labour needed in producing plantation crops all over the world.
ISBN 1-870518-18-7 Paperback £11.99

PROSPERO'S RETURN? Historical Essays on Race, Culture and British Society. By Paul Rich. In this wide-ranging collection of essays, the author explores the nature and meaning of race and racism in British society and the nature of British and English national identity.
ISBN 1-870518-40-3 Paperback £8.95

KING OF THE CARNIVAL AND OTHER STORIES. By Willi Chen. A unique collection of short stories from the Caribbean, capturing the violence, trickery, pathos and racial comedy of Trinidadian society.
ISBN 1-870518-12-8 Paperback £5.95

THE OPEN PRISON. A novel by Angus Richmond. The story of Angela, a sensitive and disturbed child, growing up on the estate of her white guardian in British Guiana, is slowly and painfully awakened to a society in turmoil, in which both black and white are struggling to reassert their roles during the First World War.
ISBN 1-870518-25-X Paperback £4.95

SPEECHES BY ERROL BARROW. Edited by Yussuff Haniff. A collection of speeches made by the late Barbadian Prime Minister, showing Barrow as a true Caribbean man, fighting for the region's independent identity. This book is now recommended reading in most Barbadian schools.
ISBN 1-870518-70-5 Hardback £10.95

THE REGGAE FILES. By Gordon C. A collection of interviews with reggae superstars from Jamaica and Britain who speak about the influence of Jamaican politics, Rastafarian ideas and the black British experience on the creation of their music.
ISBN 1-870518-03-9 Paperback £6.95

COOLIE ODYSSEY. By David Dabydeen. This book, Dabydeen's second collection of poetry, probes the experience of diaspora, the journeying from India to the Caribbean then to Britain, dwelling on the dream of romance, the impotence of racial encounter and the metamorphosis of language.
ISBN 1-870518-01-2 Paperback £3.95

PASSION AND EXILE. By Frank Birbalsingh. A wide ranging collection of essays that offer an illuminating commentary on the literary and social history of the English speaking Caribbean.
ISBN 1-870518-16-0 Paperback £7.95

THE WEB OF TRADITION: USES OF ALLUSION IN V.S. NAIPAUL'S FICTION. By Dr John Thieme. An exciting study of one of the Caribbean's major and most controversial novelists, V.S. Naipaul, who has won several of the world's literary prizes including the Booker Prize.
ISBN 1-870518-30-6 Paperback £6.95

Enquiries: Hansib Publishing Limited, Third Floor, Tower House, 141-149 Fonthill Road, London N4 3HF Tel: 0171-281 1191.

Book trade distribution: Turnaround Distribution, 27 Horsell Road, London N5 1XL Tel: 0171-609 7836/7.